Be A Phenomenal Listener

Master the Key to All Effective Communication – Listening

By David Leads

Legal Disclaimer

Table of Contents

Introduction

The process of communicating involves both the sending and receiving of messages delivered through various channels and methods. Many of the messages we receive on a daily basis are coursed through text or digital format, but a vast majority involves our listening skills, often intricately connected to visual communication as well.

Our ears, the instruments used for listening, are very important to our ability to pick up and decipher various sounds, noises, and signals sent via sound waves. According to a group called Get In Front Communications, about 55 per cent of the message we receive is obtained from watching facial expressions or body gestures, 38 per cent from the tone used to deliver the message, and 7 per cent from the actual words said.

Why is listening an art? It is a combination of skills and acquired know-how of the most effective practices from both auditory and visual cues. As mentioned above, it involves more than just listening with your ears, but also picking up on what is actually being said through visual images, facial expressions, and mental reasoning. Just like any art or skill, listening can be developed over time, but it has to be understood and adjusted in order to become as effective as possible to the listener.

Listening and hearing are two different things

Studies show that on average, we hear about 125-250

words every minute. This average, of course, varies depending on the time of the day and the activities that you are performing. For instance, you are likely hearing more words spoken when sitting at a lecture, attending a meeting, or driving down the freeway listening to a radio talk show, as compared to when you are sitting at home relaxing with a cup of coffee, or jogging around the park in the early evening.

Have you ever heard someone say, "You're not *listening* to me!" You try to reason and say that you were, but more than likely the reason why you were told this line is because you *were* hearing what the other person was saying, but not really *listening* to the message. The two are different from each other in as far as focus is concerned; hearing is a more passive activity directed towards the general source of sounds, while listening requires a more conscious effort to receive the intended message from the source.

Think about your daily routine for a moment, and you can easily see the difference between hearing and listening, and how we actually use both of these throughout the day depending on what we are doing or what we want to achieve. The first thing you probably hear in the morning is your alarm (and it's also possibly one of those sounds you don't like to hear). Many people have clock radios, where the local news talk station comes on as their alarm. Others reach for their mobile phone and check for text messages, missed calls, e-mails, or voice mail.

As you get ready for the day, you are switching between hearing and listening while preparing breakfast, getting dressed, waking up the kids and getting them ready for school, or getting your stuff together for a big presentation at work. For instance, you probably hear the drone of the morning news in the background and pay little attention to it, but as soon as the weather or traffic update comes on, you listen more intently, perhaps even stopping to look at the TV or turn up the volume so you can plan your day. You might only *hear* the stock updates, but *listen* to the sports scores, or vice versa depending on what you are more interested in or which information is more relevant to you.

At work, effectively switching between hearing and listening can make you more efficient and productive as you go about your daily tasks. Hearing the office chitchat and banter and choosing to ignore it can save you from being distracted and ending up with several unproductive minutes. Meanwhile, intently listening to directions or guidelines will let you know how to handle an upcoming work-related situation or a new process being adopted.

In our interpersonal relationships, we are more valued by our loved ones, friends, family, and others in our circle when we are good listeners. How often have you experienced being too distracted by work or business problems, or other worries regarding various problems you are dealing with, and then getting complaints from your spouse, partner, kid, or friends that you are not really there with them at the moment? On the other hand, someone who is a good listener and knows how to tune everything out and just focus on what loved ones are saying shows that he or she values interpersonal relationships and their enrichment.

According to Get In Front Communications, very few people (less than 2 per cent of the general population) go through some type of formal training related to listening skills. But, that is not really a major obstacle that can prevent you from getting the most out of your listening efforts. It does take time and a lot of practice, but if you are set on being an effective listener, there are various steps you can take personally and integrate into your daily routines and preparations in order to develop best listening practices.

Taking time to enhance the art of listening can lead to significant improvements in your personal, professional, and interpersonal endeavors. As you develop your ability to really understand and apply proper action to the information that you receive, there are benefits that can have positive impact on your time management, task planning, resource management, and leadership abilities. Effective listening makes you adept at decoding messages, taking only what is important to you and to your situation, and enabling you to carry out the appropriate action.

A passage from the English Standard Version Bible found in James 1:22 states, *"But be doers of the word, and not hearers only..."* This is the goal of effective listening: to spur the right action in the listener, instead of just being a passive hearer who does not do anything with the message he received. Success in listening will be achieved when its purpose is clarified, and the right plan of action is then taken.

Chapter 1 – The Different Types of Listening

Listening may be different from plain and simple hearing, but there are also different types of listening depending on their purpose and the techniques involved. Let's take a look at some of the basic kinds of listening, keeping in mind that in our daily interactions some of these may overlap or are interconnected as we aim to be effective listeners.

Discriminative listening

The simplest and most basic kind of listening is discriminative. This starts from childhood, and discriminative listening is directed more towards the source of the sounds, the type of sounds being produced, and differentiating these sounds from the general stimuli. When a child begins to make a distinction between the voice of his mother and father, and reacts differently to them, he or she is using and enhancing discriminative listening.

As we get older and are exposed to more sounds and the complexities of language, discriminative listening also plays a big role in deciphering the nuances of messages that we listen to. Discriminative listening enables us not only to be able to tell the gender of the speaker, or how many people are actually talking, but also recognize the differences in accents, stresses, and emphasized sounds. We also use discriminative listening when we listen for cues in the speaker's voice or tone to determine emotions or understated feelings.

For instance, if you have a very close friend whom you

speak to on a daily basis, you can immediately tell by the tone of their voice, or perhaps other cues such as a slower pace of speaking, if they have something on their mind. Even if they tell you that they are fine, you can likely deduce that they have a problem or distraction just from how they are speaking, and this is part of discriminative listening.

Comprehensive listening

Another type of listening is used to understand the actual message received, and this is called comprehensive listening. From the term itself (*comprehend* or *comprehension*), this kind of listening makes use of analysis and evaluation to interpret the message that was delivered. The process of comprehension hinges on a number of factors, which may include knowledge of the material or subject matter, personal experiences, or comparative examples, among others.

How we comprehend what we listen to can vary from the interpretation of the person sitting right next to us, even if it is the exact same message. This is because we come from different backgrounds, hence we are drawing from a wide variety of experiences to draw conclusions or infer what we listen to. If you want to expand and enhance your comprehensive listening skills, it is important to be open to various perspectives and sources of learning, equipping yourself with as much information as you can to be able to effectively comprehend what you hear.

Critical listening

Closely connected to comprehensive listening is critical listening, which judges, evaluates, and/or forms opinions on the message heard. Critical listening juxtaposes the message with any existing rules, guidelines, or mores, and then evaluates or assesses positive or negative aspects, understanding the strengths and weaknesses of the points and arguments presented, in order to formulate a stand.

Although the speaker or message source may be using different visual cues, facial expressions, or body gestures, when one is attempting to be a critical listener it often requires looking past the visual cues and simply focusing on the content of the message being delivered. There are instances where visual imagery can be used to distract from the true intent or agenda of what is being said, so critical listening zeroes in on judging the actual meaning rather than the presentation.

When we sit through a sales pitch or listen to a business proposal, critical listening is used to sift through the information presented and figure out the pros and cons, visualize possibilities and potential obstacles, and ultimately come to a decision on what would be the necessary plan of action or if the ideas presented will be accepted. Much of our day-to-day planning and decision-making, as well as attempts to mediate or resolve interpersonal conflicts, require varying levels of critical listening as messages are scrutinized and judgments are made.

Biased listening

When a person is only listening to what they want to hear, or only receiving and analyzing based on his or her own notions and perspectives, this is referred to as biased listening. Biased listening leaves little to no room for arguments, presentation of differing opinions, and evaluation of points or evidence supporting the contrary position. Rather, biased listening only seeks to reinforce what one is already set on believing.

Actually, biased listening does involve evaluation, because the listener will need to analyze and sift through the information presented in order to know which ones support the stereotypes and preconceived notions he already espouses. However, more often than not biased listening also leads to distorting facts or ideas in order to fit one's personal agenda instead of allowing differing ideas in the formulation of a final analysis.

Sympathetic listening

From the word *sympathy*, which means to share or commiserate with someone's feelings, sympathetic listening involves giving ear to the speaker's situation and attempting to show understanding, compassion, and support. Sympathetic listening plays a big part in many of our interpersonal relationships; it is the type of listening that is often integral to bonds formed or strengthened between friends and loved ones.

When a friend or loved one calls to let us know of a

difficult situation they may be experiencing, such as job loss, failure of a business venture, divorce or marital separation, illness, or a death in the family, we make use of sympathetic listening to let the person know that we stand with them and understand what they are going through. This type of listening may involve sharing one's personal anecdotes regarding similar circumstances, but oftentimes, simply holding the speaker's hand or nodding in agreement is sufficient.

Empathetic or therapeutic listening

Empathetic listening attempts to understand the perspective or experience of the speaker by placing oneself in that circumstance, temporarily letting go of one's own opinions or feelings toward the matter. Empathy may not seem that much different from sympathy, but in reality they are not so similar. While sympathy takes the listener to the level of the speaker and allows for shared emotions or feelings, empathy calls for intellectually positioning the listener without losing their own ability to understand the circumstance and evaluate the next step.

When counselors, therapists, and other professionals hold sessions with their patients or clients, they utilize empathetic or therapeutic listening in order to fully understand what the client is going through and suggest the appropriate treatment or resolution. Empathetic listening is achieved by asking series of questions and follow-up queries that bring to light the different dynamics that pertain to the speaker's experience.

Chapter 2 – Reasons to Improve Your Listening Skills

While most of us would rather be talking or enjoy being the one speaking, we stand to learn more and absorb more life-enriching information by developing our skills in listening. Aside from being an effective listener who is aware of various situations and has the ability to correctly interpret and act on messages, developing listening skills allows one to have more positive, meaningful, and impactful relationships with the people around him, as well as gain an advantage in professional settings.

You can compare your listening abilities to any body part or muscle group that is worked out and exercised regularly in order to become stronger and more toned. Since our ears, eyes, and brain all play their roles in the listening process, they are all part of this "muscle group" that you will need to regularly work out as you develop better habits and strategies in listening.

There are many benefits to improving your listening skills, and they are advantageous to you regardless of your age, background, or current standing in life. When you enhance your listening abilities, you also pave the way for more improvements in other key areas of your personal and professional life because effective listening often plays a role in success across disciplines.

Listening in learning

Students of all ages need to hone the listening strategies that are best suited for their needs, and develop these techniques in order to maximize the learning that they get. As a matter of fact, children already develop their listening and recognition of different sounds long before their first day in class. Much of the preschool and early elementary years are crucial to a child's learning abilities and comprehension, including phonics and other components of language.

High school and college students are expected to have already developed more independence and initiative in their listening comprehension and attentiveness. It is in these faster, more independent learning environments, however, when deficiencies or areas for improvement in listening are often highlighted. Students who have identified their own strategies for effective listening would have considerably fewer difficulties in understanding lessons, participating actively in discussions, asking pertinent questions, and applying their knowledge to real life situations.

Learning, of course, is not confined to the classroom or academic institution. People never stop learning, and the person who wants to avoid monotony or aims for continued improvement and opportunities will be presented with countless learning situations. This could be undergoing intensive training for a new job or a promotion; studying the ins and outs of an entrepreneurial venture; or even just listening to instructions for a do-it-yourself home improvement project.

Listening and learning go hand in hand. It is impossible to learn without listening, so if you are a dedicated learner, you stand to absorb and apply more important information with the enhancement of your skills in listening.

Listening in the communication process

Have you ever thought about how many people you communicate with on a daily basis aside from your family, the people you live with, or those you work with? Our day-to-day communication is not restricted to our inner circle only. Rather, plenty of situations present themselves each day that require us to communicate with others, and effective listening can help us benefit more from these situations.

When you talk to your financial advisor, bank teller, stockbroker, or insurance agent, they may be sharing some excellent advice or suggestions that could reap great financial rewards for you. If you are listening intently and using the right techniques to understand the information being presented to you, you can make use of what you know for material dividends or other benefits. Poor listening habits, however, could lead you to misunderstand or completely miss out on the opportunities.

The communication process involves the mutual exchange of ideas between parties, and in today's fast-paced marketplace and its barrage of options and message sources, you need to be aware of your own skills in listening and how these can be maximized towards your goals. From the simplest communication situations, such as talking to your fitness instructor at the local gym, to the more complex consultations with your physician regarding a medical condition, listening effectively and being able to come up with a timely analysis of the message all allow for successful interaction.

Listening in relationships

Our interpersonal relationships range from the most basic to the most challenging. You may have heard people say that in relationships, communication lines should be kept open. Now, many people erroneously mistake this to always being free to speak your mind regarding an issue or situation. What many neglect, however, is the fact that speaking is only one part of communicating; listening comprises a larger part.

How well do you listen to your partner? If you find yourself missing out on important schedules or dates, or constantly forgetting to take care of an errand requested by your spouse or partner, you may need to assess your listening habits and your ability to not only hear the message, but listen to it effectively and put it in your memory. Effective listening can also help to avoid many of the usual conflicts that arise in any relationship or partnership between two people, especially as both parties learn to listen for clues and become open to ideas other than their own.

Parents also need to be good listeners to their children. Children have different personalities, emotional touch points, and interests, and as they grow up the way that parents deal with their needs and development also evolves. Listening to your children talk about the things they are learning and exploring every day, the activities they are involved in at school or elsewhere, and what they are doing with their friends and peers not only helps you in your listening strategies as a parent, but also helps you understand and look for clues or hints at potential issues that you will need to deal with as you assist in their development.

They may not show it or verbally express it all the time, but children need the attention and listening ear of their parents. It is a sign of security to them, and helps to boost their self-esteem and confidence in their own abilities. A child that has developed open communication with his or her parents will likely grow up to be confident in his or her skills, and is better able to manage criticism and attention from society in general. On the other hand, children who do not feel like they have someone to listen to at home will seek that validation elsewhere, and this can lead to feelings of inadequacy or doubting one's self-esteem if not resolved properly.

Letting children know that their thoughts and feelings are important enough to be listened to builds their perception of themselves and their abilities. Children need their parents or other responsible adults to listen to their thoughts and help them navigate their experiences growing up. For instance, as kids go through their first feelings of achievement, victory, loneliness, defeat, rejection, sadness, excitement, and other emotions, they need to be assured that these are all part of a person's life, and they will benefit from the guidance and proper management of these circumstances. On the contrary, kids who lack someone who can listen to their feelings and how to deal with these properly can develop wrong motivations, views, and defense mechanisms carried on to adulthood.

Our friendships are also relationships that require effective listening skills. In fact, for a lot of people it is their friendships that allow them more opportunities to confide as well as to lend an ear to situations or perspectives that are mutually shared. This is because we choose our circle of friends, while family connections are mostly established by birth or legal status. With our peers, we have gravitated towards each other likely because of common interests or life circumstances, and the potential for deeper, more meaningful bonds and lines of communication are endless.

When a friend asks to see you to talk about a problem he or she is going through, effective listening will recognize if you are needed to simply sympathize or empathize with the situation, or help sift through the realities and figure out the best possible solution. A person who is considered a good friend is more often than not thought of as a great listener as well. Friends trust you and consider you as someone they can confide in when they know that you are a good listener.

In our relationships with a spouse, partner, child, family member, or friend, it is often necessary to also listen with the heart aside from the ears. Listening with your heart means recognizing that as you listen to the other person, you are not only absorbing information or getting the hard facts, but also becoming more intricately a part of that person's life, forging a deeper bond than you already have with them.

Effective listening is very important in resolving both potential and ongoing conflicts or tensions in our personal relationships. Sitting down and offering to just listen to what other people want to say signals that you are willing to hash everything out and figure out the best possible solution for everyone, instead of just having it your way or resolving it the only way you know how. As you listen effectively, you also begin to see other perspectives better and this leads to a balanced approach to the problem at hand.

Listening in the workplace

The workplace is a venue where people of different personalities, backgrounds, goals, and interests are grouped together and interact every day. The potential for tension, misunderstanding, and conflict exists, but if effective listening and good communication skills are harnessed properly the negative outcomes can be minimized, fostering an open and healthy exchange of ideas instead.

Those in leadership hold the key to establishing a workplace that encourages good listening and attention to the ideas of others. Dynamic, progressive companies and enterprises often have, at the helm, owners, entrepreneurs, and executives who are willing to listen to ideas and suggestions formulated within the organization or outside. They realize that as the organization or enterprise grows, it becomes impossible for just one person to keep an eye on everything that goes on, much less effectively handle problems that call for immediate resolution, and they need to listen to the advice and solutions presented by others around them that can be trusted and have the interest of the entire organization in mind.

Whatever your position, title, or role may be within the enterprise or company, you stand to gain a lot from developing your listening skills in this area of your professional life. Good listening strategies allow you to absorb a lot of ideas for improvement, as well as best practices from colleagues that can help you take your work performance to the next level and increase productivity. You enrich yourself through ideas culled from the experiences of others around you who may have been there longer than you have, and this also allows you to avoid pitfalls they had in the past.

If resolving conflicts or coming up with solutions to problems is an integral part of your responsibility in the company or professional organization, your listening skills will assist you in formulating a fair, balanced strategy that considers all sides or proposals presented, with the goal of creating the best possible resolution for all parties involved. Employees often complain that those in upper management do not listen to their concerns, and many times this is because they do not feel that their concerns, legitimate as they may be, are being addressed or acknowledged as part of the organization's focus. Listening to these concerns will most likely lead to a workplace that is more productive and maximizes available resources.

Ongoing training and development are essential to the growth and relevance of any company or enterprise. Improving your listening skills will allow you to learn the information, trends, practices, or strategies that you need to further develop your role within the organization and improve your performance. Training classes, seminars, conferences, industry conventions, calibrations, and other professional training situations require active and effective listening. In the workplace, meetings and group huddles are also situations that call for your focused listening.

As you can see from the examples mentioned above, improving how you listen to and analyze messages not only develops one specific area of your life, but permeates all of your interpersonal dealings and interactions as well. Investing time and effort into maximizing your own listening techniques can lead to a more enriched, productive, and meaningful life experience that transforms you into a better individual.

Chapter 3 – Focus Your Listening

Much like how you focus your sight on something when you are keenly observing or monitoring a person or situation, you can also train your ears and your mind to focus your listening on someone or something. This is a skill that is beneficial especially because you do not always have control over the immediate surroundings and the ambient noise or other potential distractions.

Focus requires a conscious effort to ignore other stimuli that could grab your listening attention and cause you to lose part of the message or come across as inattentive and disinterested. There are some techniques you can employ that can greatly assist you in maintaining listening focus throughout the conversation or message delivery, minimizing distractions, interruptions, and the potential loss of key ideas or concepts.

Eye contact

It is easier to maintain your focus on the source of the message when you maintain eye contact. Looking directly at the person speaking gives your brain the signal to also hone in on what the speaker is saying, so you also block out other things that may be happening around you, even situations or people that may not necessarily be making a lot of sound but can still cause you to get distracted.

Of course, maintaining eye contact during the conversation also signals to the speaker that you are giving him or her your undivided attention, and that you do care about what they are saying. Think for a moment and try to remember an instance when you were talking to someone and they were constantly glancing around, looking over your shoulder, or even looking at their feet (or worse, their watch!). How did it make you feel? Did it make you want to keep saying what you were saying, or did you want to just stop because they did not seem to want to listen anyway?

Looking at the speaker's eyes lets him or her know that you are right there with them in the conversation, that you are not thinking of anything else, and you care enough to let go of other distractions and stimuli in order to fully understand what they are saying. People appreciate this as this makes the flow of communication more effective, meaningful, and enriching. More importantly, when it is your turn to speak, they will likely give you the same respect and attention you afforded them.

In a group setting, such as a seminar or lecture, or when you attend a religious service, it may not be possible to establish eye contact if you are very far from the speaker; also, the person talking may also be establishing eye contact with the entire group or class. Simply focusing your attention on the speaker directly would be enough to help you maintain focus. Looking around not only allows you to get distracted, but this can also be very obvious to the speaker especially if you are in a very visible position.

Lose the distractions

There are stimuli, situations, and attention-grabbers

that are beyond your control. But there are also potential distractions that you have complete control over, and losing these distractions before or during your conversation or listening activity will make way for a more effective reception of the message. These possible distractions include gadgets, unnecessary comments, interruptions, and side conversations.

Our mobile devices these days have become very much a part of all of our activities. A lot of people walk around with their smartphone or tablet in their hand, constantly checking for messages or updates. In addition, music and entertainment players, as well as handheld game consoles, also take much of people's attention. If you need to focus your listening on someone, you need to put away your phone or tablet for a few minutes and give your undivided attention to whoever is speaking. Best is to place it in a pocket or bag too, rather than leaving it on a table or out in the open.

Now, it is also true that in many of our daily interactions we use our mobile devices to actually enhance the conversation or even note important reminders or schedules, and that is fine. If the use of your device is related to the ongoing communication, then it is productive and can make you a more efficient listener. However, if what you are doing on your mobile device has nothing to do with the communication at hand, then it is a distraction and is not helping you maximize your listening, so make sure to put it away.

The same can be applied to group settings. In many classrooms, seminars, or training programs and lectures, participants are encouraged to use their tablets, laptops, or other devices to take notes, participate in conversations, or look at materials and supplementary visuals that go with the content. However, if someone is checking personal e-mails, carrying out a non-related conversation via IM or text, or just browsing other sites that are not related to what is going on, then this is a distraction and gets in the way of listening effectively.

Have you ever talked to or sat next to someone who had a habit of making side comments that are not constructive or beneficial to the conversation? These remarks are another kind of distraction that you can avoid. Aside from the fact that unrelated side comments can come across as very rude to the speaker, they also take away your attention from the speaker and what he or she is saying. At the same time, side comments and unnecessary remarks are not only distracting to you and the person speaking, but also to other people around you who are trying to listen and pay attention.

Meanwhile, within group settings such as class lectures, seminars, or business meetings, side conversations and interruptions are common distractions that interfere with effective listening. This happens when two or more of the participants carry on their own conversation instead of paying attention to the speaker, lecturer, or trainer. These side discussions sometimes start because of something that was said that the listeners may have found interesting or humorous and wanted to discuss further among themselves. Other times, it could be because of boredom or restlessness, especially if the session has become long and tedious.

These side conversations and interruptions, however, should be avoided if you want to make the most out of listening. There could be crucial or important message points, which you will miss out on if you are carrying on your own discussion with a friend or the person next to you. Also, your discussion could be disturbing others around you who are trying to listen, not to mention distracting to whoever is speaking. In a smaller setting, even hushed tones or whispers can be loud enough to distract others or cause the speaker to lose focus on what he or she is saying.

Gadgets, unnecessary remarks, and side conversations are interruptions that you often have control of, and if you are intent on maximizing listening opportunities and absorbing as much information as you can for personal enhancement, these distractions should not be allowed to sidetrack your goal.

Pay attention to tone and delivery

In verbal communication, the delivery and tone of the message are also significant components especially for the listener who desires to fully understand what is being said. Delivery and tone would include inflections, pitch, volume, speed, and other techniques employed both consciously and unconsciously.

There are many instances where you will need to focus your listening not only on the words you are hearing, but how they are being said, in order to have a full grasp and proper comprehension of the message. One primary example of this is the use of sarcasm, which is defined by Merriam-Webster Dictionary as "the use of words that mean the opposite of what you really want to say especially in order to insult someone, to show irritation, or to be funny." When a person asks a question that is obviously inane or unnecessary, the speaker can answer with a satirical "Yes" or "No", but the hearer can surmise sarcasm because of the tone in the speaker's voice. While a common "Yes" or "No" answer may have a downward inflection in the speaker's tone, a satirical tone would be upward, almost like a question, with an obviously condescending emphasis.

Tone and delivery are used everyday in a whole range of situations. At home, when a mother asks her child to pick up his toys for the first time, she might say, "Billy, pick up your toys please." After several minutes, if she sees that no action has been done, she might say, "Billy, I said **pick up your toys now.**" Between the two statements, there is very little variance, but what has changed? The stress in her voice that emphasized the last five words in the sentence, letting Billy know exactly what she needed him to do.

Focusing on tone, vocal techniques, and delivery of the message can greatly help you in deciphering what you are listening to. At the same time, they can also assist you in remembering key points of the message, as vocal emphasis and stress often highlight important parts of a lecture, presentation, or conversation. If you can remember *how* something was said, it may help you to recall what was said later on.

Remember body gestures

Body language is another component of verbal and nonverbal communication often employed to deliver the message in a clearer, more dramatic fashion, or simply to accentuate one's emotions or feelings and make sure they come across to the listener. Gestures would include hand movements, facial expressions, and movements of the head, eyes, shoulders, and other parts of the speaker's body.

Some bodily gestures and movements are done voluntarily as part of the communication process. The speaker may use his hands to signal towards an object he wants listeners to look at, or to motion the size, length, or direction of movement included in his message. Other forms of gestures or facial expressions are involuntary or are immediate reactions to either the content of the message being said, or surrounding stimuli.

Body gestures and facial reactions help the listener to decipher the emotions or feelings of the speaker. Emotions such as surprise, anger, grief, joy, frustration, embarrassment, excitement, and other basic feelings are easily observed through facial and bodily expressions. They also highlight certain points of the message that may help with later memory recall.

There are also times when the speaker's body movements or facial reactions somehow deliver a different message that you may need to pay attention to, conveying something else other than what is being spoken. For instance, when you ask someone how their day was, it is almost customary for the other person to reply with a number of variations of, "It was fine" or "It was good". But judging from their gestures and facial expressions, coupled with inflection or tone, you can tell if it was really good, or not too well, or perhaps just so-so.

A shrug of the shoulders, a downward glance, eyes that look fleetingly from left to right, hands that move through one's face or hair, all of these gestures may indicate that while the person you are talking to says they are fine, you may need to probe a little further in order to get them to open up about how they really feel. On the other hand, an exuberant smile, hands clapping excitedly, or a little pep in the person's step might mean they have something exciting or joyous to share with you about what happened to their day, giving you signals on what questions to ask further.

There are many signals and communication hints that you can glean from focusing not only on the words of the person speaking, but also their body movements. You will become an even more effective and responsive listener and communication partner by paying close attention to nonverbal actuations that help to more efficiently absorb the message being conveyed in its totality.

Chapter 4 – Effective Listening

Listening may seem to a lot of people as a passive activity that does not require much effort or attention in order to engage in. Now, while there are certainly some types of listening activities that are more passive in nature, effective listening required in much of our daily tasks in the home, school, workplace, and other relationships and efforts do require our full attention span and focus on comprehension.

It is important to remember that the reason behind aspiring to improve one's listening skills and enhancing efficiency in communication is not only for personal development and knowledge, but also to become a more responsive and engaging participant in the process of communication, whether you are talking to your spouse or children, making plans with your business partners or colleagues, catching up with friends, or attending a work-related seminar or industry convention. A good listener would have the advantage of being a better speaker as well, because he understands the material or content, knows how to respond accurately, and has a comprehensive grasp of what has already been communicated and where the conversation should be headed next.

Talk less, listen more

The effective listener knows that in order to understand what is being communicated, he or she will need to set aside the personal urge to talk right away, giving way for the other speaker or speakers to say what they need to say first. This makes the listener aware of where everyone is coming from, what the various perspectives are regarding the subject matter being discussed, and how the conversation will benefit from everyone's viewpoints.

Listening effectively comes with an understanding that there is a proper time for everything, and at this point in time it would be more beneficial to speak less and to simply absorb the ideas or messages being presented. When we hold off on talking, we also avoid many mistakes that come from blurting out a reaction based on a partial message or statement that we heard. Have you ever had a moment where you literally spoke too soon in reaction to what another person was saying, only to find out when you finally got the full message that what you initially said was wrong?

When we talk less, we also allow our minds to fully comprehend the message and avoid jumping to hasty conclusions or allowing our prejudices and personal biases to get in the way of listening. Allowing others to completely give us their perspective or viewpoint creates a communication flow that is respectful and generous, understanding that differences in backgrounds, opinions, and experiences make human interaction more enriching.

There are valuable contributions and focus points from the speaker or speakers that you stand to miss out on if you cut them short or interrupt their message. People reveal a lot about themselves and what they have learned or experienced when they are talking, and giving them your listening ear allows you to benefit from their experiences. You just might find yourself being exposed to a whole new perspective on an idea, process, or standpoint that you have always seen one way, and this makes you a more well rounded individual in the long run.

Of course, when people recognize you as a respectful and attentive listener, they will also be more likely to reciprocate with the same attention and courtesy when it is your turn to speak. In fact, when people you converse with know that you have afforded them the proper time to air their side, they will likely be the ones to ask for your input on the matter because they know that you have taken the time and effort to understand their message, as opposed to someone who is just waiting for the slightest pause in order to butt in and take over the conversation.

Ask questions

The right questions at the right time can help the listener clarify or better understand something that the speaker has said. Depending on the situation you are in, questions may be appropriate immediately or at a later time. In a personal, one-on-one conversation with a family member, friend, or colleague, questions are usually welcome and appropriate when asked right away, as long as you keep in mind not to abruptly cut short or interrupt whoever is talking.

As an example, when your spouse, partner, or child mentions something that you were not previously aware of or may be confusing to you, asking for clarification helps you to continue listening to the rest of the message with the right perspective in mind. On the other hand, feigning understanding when you are really confused about something mentioned midway through the conversation might result in the wrong conclusions later on.

Meanwhile, there are other times when your queries may have to be set aside for a more appropriate setting. In a large business seminar or lecture, speakers usually are given free rein to talk during their time period, after which a question and answer portion is commenced so listeners can pitch their queries regarding the talk. For this setting, it would be helpful to take down notes and write your questions so you do not forget. You might find that some of your initial questions are eventually answered after you listen to the rest of the talk, so you no longer need to ask them at the end.

In classroom or academic settings, the forum for questions may also vary. Some professors, trainers, or speakers encourage participants to raise their hands when they have questions, and they give way to these queries even in the middle of their lecture. Other speakers or educators prefer questions to be asked towards the end of the presentation, or even privately once the class or session is over. Whatever the case may be, it would be helpful to know beforehand what the guideline is.

At the workplace, business meetings or office huddles have their own established practices when it comes to the flow of communication and when to ask clarifying questions. Some meetings are virtual free-for-all sessions where executives, managers, and staff are encouraged to speak their minds right away when it comes to pitching ideas, discussing suggestions, and coming up with solutions to workplace concerns. Other speakers or executives may prefer that listeners raise their hands first before asking questions, or hold off until the end of the talk. Again, regardless of the circumstance, respecting boundaries and avoiding unnecessary interruptions should be the rule of thumb.

How do you know what questions to ask? The right questions clarify a point and make it easier to comprehend, rather than adding to the confusion or causing the conversation to veer towards a completely unrelated topic. Queries should lead towards a resolution and a plan of action. If there are other people also asking questions, you should also pay attention to what they are asking, and the answers being given, as the questions you may have in your head may already be addressed. When you ask a question that has already been answered, it tells the speaker that you were not listening to the answers already given.

Empathize with the speaker

A helpful strategy that can transform how you listen effectively is the utilization of empathy with the speaker. Empathy involves putting yourself mentally and emotionally in the speaker's perspective, looking at the subject matter from the speaker's point of view, taking your own views and prejudices away to fully grasp where the speaker is coming from. Empathizing with the speaker allows you to reconstruct the idea or message of the speaker for complete engagement and comprehension.

Some people erroneously perceive empathic listening as readily agreeing to anything and everything that the speaker is saying, regardless of logic, reasoning, or the facts involved. This is the wrong approach to this communication strategy. A lot of times, it may seem quite convenient to just agree with everything that the speaker is saying, for instance, if you have a family member or friend who is complaining about something that was done by another person which, in their eyes, was wrong or unfair. It's tempting to just take their side and say, "Yes, you're right, they should not have done that". But without really taking time to go through the facts and get to the bottom of what really happened, this does not resolve anything and may even compound the situation.

Empathy means going through the events that the speaker is narrating, taking time to hash out the details and ask clarifying questions as needed. By seeking to recreate the timeline and what the people involved were going through at the time, you can gain a better understanding of what transpired, what may have led to the conflict, and what could have been done differently. Best of all, empathic listening will allow you to come up with the best possible solution for all involved.

One strength of empathic listening is placing the listener in a non-judgmental, neutral position that will allow him or her to objectively look at the details and understand the speaker without making biased conclusions. As human beings, we are often easily affected by personal emotions or feelings, and if not managed properly, these personal prejudices can cloud our own judgments and affect how we relate to what the speaker is saying, especially if the person speaking is highly emotional at the time.

Empathic or reflective listening is a technique often employed by professional counselors, therapists, or psychologists in their sessions with clients. This strategy allows the professional to go through the events and relate to their client while not losing sight of the hard truths in the matter. Also, reflective listening skills are valuable in the area of problem solving, because going back and recreating each step will often identify key actions or causes of issues or conflicts, and become the key to finding a solution to the problem.

Be patient

Our contemporary society is geared towards getting results as quickly and conveniently as possible. Modern devices such as smartphones, tablets, and notebooks used with lightning speed Internet connections provide users with information at their fingertips, retrievable within just a few seconds, for their consumption. Consumers value retailers or establishments that promise quickly prepared meals or fast delivery service, or choose to shop online where selections are quicker and priority shipping is offered. Everything is designed for on-the-go individuals with little time for waiting, and even the smallest window of delay can be seen as a major inconvenience.

As a listener, patience is an important tool that you should always have if your goal is to become a more efficient communication participant. Patience will make you more adaptive and flexible to the needs of the people around you with whom you communicate constantly. In the flow of communication, not everything can be understood and resolved within just a short period of time. There are instances when you will need to practice patience and understanding in order to be an engaged and efficient listener.

Parents, in particular, know fully well the importance of patiently listening to and guiding their children as they go through the various stages of growing up. When kids relate their experiences or tell their parents about their feelings or emotions, parents have to look beyond the occasional rambling or incoherent sentences or ideas due to the still-developing communication and language skills of the young ones.

Children are surprisingly aware of the patience and attention span of their parents and other grown-ups around them. They can tell if you really care about what they are saying, or if your mind is completely elsewhere and you are just absently nodding or uttering responses. Because acceptance and validation from their adult influences are important to children, it is a must to be patient as they try to communicate their experiences and feelings.

An attitude of patience and understanding is also valuable in other listening endeavors. If you are in school or training for a new job, you will inevitably experience periods of boredom or restlessness as you try to absorb the material or lesson content. But this is information that you will need later on as you advance to more complicated lessons, or as you perform your work duties, so listening patiently and trying to focus on the subject matter is not optional, but a requirement for later success.

The people that we communicate with on a daily basis have different personalities, backgrounds, and opinions, and listening to their expressions and perspectives will often require a great deal of patience on your part. Some of our family members, colleagues, business clients, and neighbors are more opinionated or vocal about their feelings, while others are more introverted and take a bit more prodding in order to open up. In either case, patience is necessary and needs to be adjusted accordingly, whether it is holding back on your immediate reactions to strong statements and waiting for the speaker to finish talking, or being more intuitive and asking leading questions to get someone to really verbalize their thoughts.

Set aside preconceived notions and prejudices

When listening, you have to be open to learning new things and going beyond the things you already know, perhaps even being challenged regarding ideas or beliefs you may have held for a long time. Efficient listening brings about learning, and part of the process of learning is the realization that there may be ideas or viewpoints that are just as valid and reasonable as the ones you hold to, but varying greatly in their basic concepts or applications.

In fact, we all know or have heard of people who are staunch believers of certain beliefs or guidelines, and who refuse to even listen to others who hold opinions or standards that are contrary to theirs. This is partly because they realize that when listening to other people who may have contrary ideas as theirs, they may be forced to challenge their own sets of beliefs, and this can be an uncomfortable reality for some.

Our own prejudices and biases stem from a variety of factors, including upbringing, environment, or prior experiences. Notions and long-held beliefs, however, should not take preeminence over continued learning and the desire to constantly expand one's horizons. Learning and development should be continuing endeavors, and one's motivation behind efficient listening is the focus on opening one's mind to new, fresh innovations and concepts.

Sticking to one's traditions, prejudices, and stock knowledge is stifling and restricts the person's potential to achieve levels of success that he or she may not even realize. On the other hand, someone who is adaptable and is open to continued learning through efficient listening would tend to be more receptive to new trends and best practices, picking up important knowledge and strategies for furthering one's goals.

Chapter 5 – The Supportive Listener

Good communication is a two-way process and involves the sharing, delivery, and reception of messages between two or more people who add valuable contributions to the conversation. As a listener, you stand to maximize the listening opportunity and also enhance the communication process by being the most supportive listener that you possibly can. This also paves the way for a clearer understanding of what is being said, as well as a more enriching interaction between speaker and listener.

Acknowledge the speaker

Have you ever experienced being in a conversation, or speaking in front of a group of people, and not feeling like anyone is listening to what you are saying? Perhaps this was because none of the participants were responding when you were asking general questions towards the audience, or you made some humorous comments that no one laughed at, or even said an emphatic statement designed for emotional impact but with no results.

The speaker will feel more confident and encouraged to continue delivering the message if he or she receives appropriate acknowledgment from the listener. Whether it is a one-on-one interaction with a friend or family member, or a small group setting such as a huddle at work, or even a seminar or training session you are attending, giving the speaker some form of acknowledgment lets him or her know that you are paying attention, you care about what they are saying, and that the interaction matters to you personally.

Acknowledgments differ depending on the situation you are in. When talking to your kids at the end of the day, or relaxing with your spouse or partner at your favorite hangout, appropriately acknowledging them would include a nod, agreeing with an enthusiastic "Yes," a playful pat on the back or supportive arm around their shoulder, or laughing or crying along with their anecdotes.

On the other hand, for group settings, acknowledging the speaker may entail you to nod in agreement to a point taken, shaking your head when hearing an unbelievable or ridiculous story, raising your head when the speaker asks for a show of hands, or applause during or after the speech.

When you are acknowledging the speaker sincerely, this also helps you to maintain your attention and focus on what is being said instead of allowing your mind to wander off or get distracted by what is happening around you. So acknowledgments not only help the speaker, but also make you a more efficient listener in the process.

Help the speaker relax

People have varying levels of speaking skills and confidence, and it helps if the listener is supportive enough to be aware of the speaker's confidence level in order to help make the experience easier. While many people struggle with public speaking or addressing a large group of people, there are also instances when even an intimate interaction or conversation can be intimidating to one or more parties involved, and the intuitive listener will need to take steps to help the speaker relax.

If you are an authority figure such as a teacher, manager, business owner, or mentor, you must be aware that your very title or position can seem intimidating to some people you interact or work with. This can make them apprehensive or hesitant to communicate honestly and directly with you. You may find that even the simplest question that you ask someone makes him or her visibly nervous, or stare at their feet or somewhere else in the room instead of looking directly at you.

It will depend largely on you to make the interaction much less nerve-wracking and intimidating for the other person by making some adjustments, perhaps to your speaking style or voice inflections, to assure the person you are talking to that the conversation matters to you and you care about what they have to say. Some facial expressions or body gestures help put the speaker at ease, such as direct eye contact, an affirmative nod, a supportive arm around their shoulder, or a firm handshake coupled with a warm smile.

When you are listening to a person who is nervous about addressing the group, a welcoming smile and direct eye contact helps put him at ease, as well as verbal agreements or acknowledgments to what they are saying. Gradually, as the speaker realizes that the audience is receptive, he or she will begin to feel more relaxed, making the communication smoother.

Another instance when you might need to do this as a

listener is when you are speaking to a child, spouse, friend, family member, or colleague who is very emotional. What the other person is saying may be hard to understand if they are extremely angry, upset, or sobbing uncontrollably. You can help them relax first by reminding them to take deep breaths, perhaps offering some water, sitting them down, and allowing them to regain control of their feelings and emotions first so they can better communicate with you.

Listen with an open mind

Speakers can tell if their audience is receptive, critical, or at least open to what is being said. Now, it may be difficult to always be receptive or agreeing to what you are hearing. There will always be instances when you disagree with certain points or content to a message being delivered, or a conversation you are participating in. But having an open mind, ready to listen to and evaluate different perspectives, shows that you value what people are saying, and that as a listener, you are open to discussion and analyzing your own views.

Listening with an open mind means removing any barriers or biases that may get in the way of fairly, objectively, reasonably discussing topics or matters with the people you are conversing with. It comes with the realization that what you think you know may not necessarily be fully accurate, or is a small component of a larger, more comprehensive picture. The reality is that very few things in the world are absolute, and there are many processes, ideas, or facts that are continually shaped by changes, societal trends, and human experiences, and listening with an open mind helps you stay in touch with new realities.

The supportive listener lends not only two ears that are ready to hear what the speaker is saying, but an open mind that is willing to learn and consider wide-ranging perspectives and recognize the value of consistently aiming for development and personal enrichment.

Don't interrupt

Being a supportive listener means not interrupting the speaker and holding off on unnecessary remarks or statements until the appropriate time. Interrupting someone is rude, and not only hinders maximum listening benefits for you, but also for others who may also be listening and trying to pay attention. At the same time, a sudden interruption can completely take the speaker off track and lose his focus, and if this has ever happened to you in the middle of an important presentation or lecture, you know that it can be difficult to recover or regain composure.

Asking questions or clarifying certain details are not necessarily interruptions, as discussed in previous chapters. Questions that are pertinent to the discussion help to make the message clearer and easier to comprehend. But they have to be timed appropriately and follow any protocol or guidelines set by the group or the speaker so it does not take the speaker from his or her element.

Interruptions such as side comments or conversations with other participants while the speaker is talking should be avoided. These are not the actions of a supportive listener, and can distract whoever is talking and make them feel that they are not being valued or listened to, disrupting healthy interaction.

Contribute to the conversation

At the other end of the spectrum, a supportive and efficient listener will have positive and meaningful contributions to make to the conversation or discussion at hand especially when input is encouraged. Contributing to the discussion shows that you paid attention to the message being delivered, and also gives you a venue to put into practice what you have learned while interacting with others.

Contributing to the discussion may be as simple as giving healthy, valuable advice to your children after they have recounted their day's activities. Children are looking for positive role models and need the guidance of their parents in understanding the different aspects of growing up, from their schoolwork and how to manage their time between homework and sports, to pursuing various interests they may have in other areas such as music, art, or reading. Giving them your thoughts and advice assures them of your support in their pursuits.

In the classroom or training environment, participants are often encouraged to participate in discussions around the subject material. Educators, trainers, and professors are aware that these conversations are a good gauge of whether their audience understood the material, and how they will respond to what they have heard. Different perspectives and approaches to the subject matter also enrich the learning process for everyone involved.

As a contributor in the workplace, regardless of your position in the company, enterprise, or organization, participants are encouraged to share their ideas, especially those that would improve current processes and approaches, or highlight best practices. The level of competition in most industries today makes it imperative for companies and members of management to source ideas, innovations, and practices from those who are on the front lines and directly familiar with the goings-on, such as staff members and employees.

Chapter 6 – Hindrances to Effective Listening

Just like any endeavor in life, improving your listening skills towards maximum efficiency and effectively will not come without its share of obstacles and challenges. But any hindrances to the ultimate goal are part and parcel of having a vision for oneself, and these challenges should not deter you from reaching for excellence. Rather, hindrances can be managed and used to build character, determination, and maturity.

Hidden agendas

Whether a hidden agenda or ulterior motive is coming from the listener, speaker, or others in the conversation, this can become a stumbling block to clear, honest, and open communication. Some participants in a discussion may make it appear that they are a part of the conversation and where it is headed, but the truth is they have other motives in mind, and once they see the opportunity to steer the conversation towards their goal, they will not hesitate to do so.

How do you overcome hidden motives or agendas in a discussion? One tactic is to look for opportune times to ask questions or clarifications that lead back to the original purpose or intent of the conversation, calmly but firmly reminding the speaker and the participants of the topic or purpose.

Egotistical perspectives

Much like hidden motives and agendas, egotistical views are also obstacles to effective communication. Some people join a discussion or conversation with the full belief that they are better than everyone else, and what they have to say or contribute should be followed by everyone else. This very self-centered perspective seeks to block or drown out other ideas or suggestions offered that are contrary or different from one's own viewpoint.

When dealing with this hindrance as a listener, you want to maintain objectivity and an open mind to the differences of opinion, but also encourage participants to respect variances and allow for different factors and variables to make the end result more productive.

Low energy, illness, or health issues

If you are dealing with health problems, an illness, or low energy due to fatigue or stress, this can get in the way of effective listening and the contribution to the communication flow. It is difficult for the mind to focus on listening to a discussion at hand when there is pain, discomfort, and other bodily abnormalities or disorders also taking its attention. In addition, there are medications that can make a person feel drowsy, or impact focus or coordination, adding to the difficulty in listening focus.

Staying healthy and being mindful of one's body and energy level should not be neglected in the effort to become a more efficient listener. All parts of the body are interconnected, and when one part is not working properly, the rest of our anatomy can feel the deficiency. Take steps to keep your body healthy and well rested, and maintain regular consultations with your physician to ensure that the body is at its optimum.

Anxiety

Anxiety takes on various forms, but in relation to listening and the communication process it is mostly seen in instances of social anxiety. This refers to an extreme, unhealthy, and often paralyzing fear of disapproval, embarrassment, or rejection by the social group, causing the person to withdraw or avoid social interactions or contributions altogether. A listener who suffers from some form of social anxiety may be hesitant to respond or share to the discussion, even if he or she is fully capable and knowledgeable, because of the fear of being wrong or ridiculed.

Professional counseling and other medical treatments may be necessary in order to deal with and manage anxiety and make the person able to function in social settings. In addition, some forms of anxiety can lead to or are symptoms of other medical conditions, so it is important that this is given the right attention and care.

Anger or personality clashes

Because people have fundamental differences in opinion, background, interests, and skills, personality clashes and disagreements cannot be completely avoided. You will inevitably get to a point where your personal perspective differs sharply with that of a partner, colleague, or friend. If this clash is not handled properly, it can lead to an undermining of the communication flow, and any headway you may have made towards efficient listening will be put to naught.

Miscommunication or misunderstandings between personalities are best resolved by simply sitting down, relaxing, taking some time to cool off, and then having a civil, respectful discussion of the differences so a compromise or solution can be worked out. If the speakers or the listeners allow emotions such as anger, frustration, and pride to take over, no resolution will be reached.

Chapter 7 – Preparing to Listen

Preparation is the key to anything we do. If you are really serious about being an effective listener and an excellent communicator, in the process, you will know how to prepare for the task at hand, arming yourself with the proper tools, conditioning, and strategies to maximize listening success and deliver the results you need.

Free your mind

Let go of any worries, considerations, or issues that are not related to the matter at hand and set them aside for later. Having too much on your mind will definitely distract you from listening intently. The mind can be taught to compartmentalize, or to set aside unnecessary details and concerns while focusing on pertinent information and facts.

Every person has a different way of freeing up the mind and "psyching up". Some people listen to music, others meditate or have a moment of solitude. Some individuals simply need to get their favorite cup of coffee or other hot beverage, along with a good book, in order to settle the mind and allow it to focus. Whatever your technique may be, use it to your advantage.

Relax your soul

Aside from physical stresses, the demands of daily life

can also take its toll on your inner being. A lot of people in modern society take time to take care of their body and get it refreshed and rejuvenated, but neglect to consider refreshing their soul and inner person as well.

Spiritual activities, retreats, motivational books or podcasts, and even quality moments with family and friends all keep the soul healthy and ready to face the challenges of daily life. If you prioritize refreshing your body, you should also remember that the soul, or the person within, needs to take a break from time to time also, and this will help you become more prepared to listen.

Healthy body, healthy listener

As mentioned in a previous chapter, a listener dealing with a myriad of health problems would have a very difficult time trying to focus on the message. Even a simple headache or aching muscles and joints can easily distract you from paying full attention to anyone. The whole body feels when parts or sections are not at their best performance.

There is a greater awareness these days regarding health and fitness, and how exercise, good nutrition, and healthy lifestyle choices contribute to a better quality of life while minimizing potential health problems. When you keep your body healthy and active, you are also making it more prepared for listening and effective communication. Think of a healthy body as a well-oiled machine that works at it is supposed to, with every part reaching full potential.

Note taking

Notes are seen as physical reminders, but there is also a memory recall or advantage that one takes from writing or typing down notes. If you are writing down something that you just heard, or typing it into your tablet or computer, there is some form of repetition happening there, and repetition definitely helps with recall.

You can use a regular paper pad and pen, a notebook, or your trusty smartphone or tablet to help you jot down important notes and remember points that are highlighted. Whatever you choose to use, keep in mind that these tools should not lead to being distracted from the main activity, which is focused listening.

Mental images and visualizations

Many people like to have visual aids and images when they are learning or listening to something, but the reality is these tools are not always readily available or utilized in listening situations. You can train your mind to more accurately remember the message by creating images or depictions in your head.

When you imagine or picture in your head what the speaker is saying, such as a personal story, an idea or process, it becomes more concrete or visible in your thinking, and this can be helpful later on as you go over what you have listened to and weigh any pros or cons, or make a decision based on the message you listened to.

Mnemonics and other memorization techniques

When there is quite a lot of information that you need to recall, you can make use of different memorization techniques and tools for easier recall. Note taking, as discussed above, is one strategy that helps people to remember information later on. Note cards are another tool, mostly used in school but can be utilized by all ages. They allow for quicker, shorter details that can be arranged in chronological or alphabetical order.

Mnemonics are also helpful in memorization. Mnemonics are techniques that make use of easy-to-remember words, lists, numerical sequences, and other strategies for easier recall. Acronyms are popular examples, such as the acronym HOMES to remember the Great Lakes (Huron, Ontario, Michigan, Erie, Superior) or ROY G. BIV for the colors of the rainbow (Red Orange Yellow Green Blue Indigo Violet). For each situation, you can create your own mnemonic in order to help you remember the relevant points of the conversation.

Chapter 8 – Taking It All In and Next Steps

The real test of efficient, effective listening is what you do with the message afterwards. What will you do with what you just listened to? It is not enough to just pay attention and get all the pertinent details that need to be processed and analyzed. An appropriate plan of action also needs to be drawn up, and the right action must take place in order for the communication impact to be felt.

Internalizing the information

How does the message relate to you, your interests, your activities, and your personal dealings? When we internalize, we assimilate the information and seek for ways to apply it to our lives. In other words, internalization means *owning* the message and making it part of your goals and direction.

When internalizing a message that you received from family members or friends, you would probably look for ways to help them out with any problem or issue, or figure out the best path to take so they can reach a goal. Internalization gives way to resolution, and this is important because the action that occurs hinges on how the information presented was absorbed and analyzed by the listener.

How does this information enrich you?

Other messages that we hear have the potential to

transform us in small or big ways if we allow them to. Perhaps it is a new perspective on an issue, or an innovative way of doing something that you have not tried before. It could also be a moment that connects you in a deeper, more meaningful way to an old friend, or to your child or spouse. Life changing, personally enriching opportunities are all around us, although sometimes we do not readily see them. In the process of communicating, recognizing these transformative messages plays a pivotal role in our own personal development.

Efficient communication can also make you a channel of positive change to the people around you whom you interact with daily. The information you listen to may be the starting point for a more involved and generous family unit, or a community that is more ecologically sustainable, or a workplace that fosters deeper cooperation between stakeholders. If you are open to the possibilities, you might be surprised at just how much potential change can occur from effective listening.

Thank you for reading this book. We hope you found this information helpful and actionable.

Please check out our other eBooks on Amazon for more resources on relationships, and visit us on the web, http://www.relationshipup.com.

Printed in Great Britain
by Amazon